Pirate adventure

A playscript
adapted from a story by
Roderick Hunt

by Jacquie Buttriss and Ann Callander

Characters

Narrator

Wilma

Wilf

Chip

Biff

This play has five speaking parts so that it can be read aloud in small groups. Sound effects can be added by children when they are familiar with the playscript but they have not been written in.

Wilma

Biff

Chip

Narrator

Wilf

Scene 1

Narrator Scene 1   'The pirate book'
Biff was looking at a book.
The book was about pirates.

Biff I don't like pirates.

Narrator Wilf and Wilma came to play.

Chip Look at the little house.

Biff It's a magic house.

Wilma Don't be silly.

Narrator They looked at the key.

Chip It's a magic key.

Wilf Don't be silly.

Narrator The key began to glow.

Scene 2

Narrator	Scene 2 'The magic house'
Biff	The magic is working.
Wilma	Oh help!

Narrator The children got smaller and smaller and smaller.

Wilf Oh no!

Wilma Oh help!

Chip I don't like this.

Biff Look at the house.

Wilf Look at the windows.

Narrator Biff went to the door.

Chip Put the key in the lock.

Wilma Open the door.

Wilf It's a magic house.

Scene 3

Narrator Scene 3 'On the sand'

Biff Look at the sand.

Chip Look at the sea.

Wilma Come on.

Narrator They ran to the sea.
Wilf picked up a shell.

Wilf Look at the shell.

Narrator Chip picked up a coconut.

Chip Look! A coconut!

Narrator Biff climbed up a tree.
Wilma went in the sea.

Wilma This is magic.

Biff What an adventure!

Narrator A pirate came up.
He looked at the children.

15

Wilf Pirates!

Chip Oh help!

Biff I don't like pirates.

Scene 4

Narrator   Scene 4   'The pirate ship'
The pirates had a boat.
They went to the pirate ship.
The children went, too.

Wilma Look at that pirate.

Chip Look at the big rope.

Wilf I'm frightened.

Narrator The pirates wanted a party.
Nobody wanted to come.

Wilma We will come to the party.

Narrator The children went to the party.

Wilf This is a good party.

Biff I like pirates.

Scene 5

Narrator Scene 5   'Time to go'

Biff The key is glowing.

Wilma It's time to go.

Chip Goodbye.

Thank you for the party.

22

Narrator Wilf looked at the little pirate hat.

Wilf What an adventure.

Biff I liked the pirates.

The end

Printed in Hong Kong